The Royal Commission on
Historical Manuscripts

Record Repositories in Great Britain

A geographical directory

London Her Majesty's
Stationery Office

© Crown copyright 1987

First published 1964
Eighth edition 1987

ISBN 0 11 440210 8

Contents

  v Preface
 vii Introduction
viii Abbreviations

      Record Repositories:
   1   England
 25   Wales
 27   Scotland
 30   Northern Ireland
 30   The Isle of Man

 31   Register offices
 32   Other useful addresses
 33   Index

Preface

In the five-year interval since the publication of the seventh edition of *Record Repositories* almost every entry has altered in some respect. Sixteen repositories have moved to new premises but the most noticeable change has been in the number of repositories which now require readers to make appointments.

The criteria for inclusion in this edition remain the same as those applied to the two previous ones. Twenty-four repositories have been added including one new county record office, five new branch offices administered by county councils and nine repositories maintained by London boroughs or metropolitan districts. The remainder comprises mainly specialist repositories which now regularly acquire historical records. Three repositories have been removed, one as a consequence of local government reorganisation in 1986. A total of 234 repositories are noticed together with details of a further twenty-four dependent institutions.

The nature of the information in the entries is also largely unchanged. The criteria for the inclusion of publications have been altered and help to other organisations has only been noticed when it includes routine staff attendance. It has also been assumed that readers are familiar with the relationship of local government branch record offices to their parent organisations. Where readers' tickets are required or admission fees charged this has, for the first time, been indicated.

The Commission is again grateful to repositories for providing the information in this edition. It has been edited for publication by JAV Rose with the assistance of BA Bamford.

BS Smith
Secretary

Quality House, Quality Court, Chancery Lane, London WC2A 1HP

1 February 1987

Introduction

Record Repositories sets out to list those institutions in the United Kingdom whose objectives include the systematic collection and preservation of written records other than those of their own administration and which also make regular provision for their public use.

The institutions concerned fall into four main categories:

(1) National record offices and libraries financed directly by central government funds

(2) Local record offices and libraries financed by local government authorities

(3) University and college libraries and departments financed mainly from central government funds through the University Grants Committee but in part by endowment and other income

(4) Special libraries and archives supported by privately or charitably endowed societies and institutions.

They are normally arranged in this order in the text, by county or region as appropriate.

In addition to the regular annual periods of closure noted, virtually all repositories are closed on public holidays and usually for one or more adjacent days, especially at Easter and between Christmas and New Year. Some repositories, as well as those listed as requesting appointments and charging an admission fee, require a letter of introduction. Readers are strongly advised to make advance enquiry on all these points.

Brief particulars of published comprehensive guides to the holdings of repositories are noted. Details of those confined to specific classes of records, typescript subject source guides and descriptions of particular collections are not noted but may be obtained from the institutions in question. Copies of the published guides and of unpublished lists of collections reported to the National Register of Archives, which is maintained by the Royal Commission on Historical Manuscripts (p 32), may be consulted in the Commission's search room.

This directory does not attempt to list the many museums and libraries which incidentally hold collections of manuscript material or the numerous other institutions and private individuals who are prepared by arrangement to make their own records available for research. Their names and addresses may be found in the reference books listed below and in many cases lists of their holdings may be consulted in the National Register of Archives. Other organisations that may be able to help students to locate papers are listed on p 32.

Libraries, museums and art galleries year book 1978-9, 1981

British archives: a guide to archive resources in the United Kingdom, by Janet Foster and Julia Sheppard, 1982, paperback edn, 1984

ASLIB Directory, Vol 1 Information sources in science, technology and commerce, 1982, *Vol 2 Information sources in the social sciences, medicine and the humanities*, 1984

Directory of British associations, 8th edn, 1986.

Abbreviations

•
Appointment required.

Photographs
Has in-house facilities to provide photographic copies. (Every repository listed can supply photocopies.)

Microfilm
Has in-house facilities to provide microfilm copies.

Repair
Has facilities for the repair of manuscripts
(★) can also in certain circumstances offer repair services to outside bodies or individuals on repayment.

P
Appointed by the Lord Chancellor as a repository for individually specified classes of public record under the provisions of section 4 of the Public Records Act 1958.

P(S)
Approved as a place of deposit for records held under the charge and superintendence of the Keeper of the Records of Scotland.

M&T
Recognised by the Master of the Rolls as a repository for manorial and tithe documents under the provisions of section 144A(7) of the Law of Property Act 1922, and section 36(2) of the Tithe Act 1936, as amended by section 7(1) of the Local Government (Records) Act 1962.

D
Designated by the bishop of a diocese as a repository for ecclesiastical records within that diocese. The name(s) of the diocese(s) and any qualifications are indicated in brackets.

ENGLAND

AVON

[1] **Bath City Record Office**
Guildhall, Bath BA1 5AW
Tel 0225 61111 ext 201
City Archivist CA Johnston

M–Th 9–1 2–5, F 9–1 2–4.30
Photographs
P

[2] **Bristol Record Office**
The Council House, College Green,
Bristol BS1 5TR
Tel 0272 266031 ext 442
City Archivist

● M–Th 9.30–4.45, F 9.30–4.15,
S 9–12. Closed last two weeks in
January
Photographs Microfilm
P M&T D (Bristol)

E Ralph, *Guide to the Bristol Archives Office*, 1971

[3] **Bristol University Library**
Tyndall Avenue, Bristol BS8 1TJ
Tel 0272 303030 ext 8014
Head of Manuscripts GE Maby

● M–F 9.15–4.45
Photographs

BEDFORDSHIRE

[4] **Bedfordshire Record Office**
County Hall, Bedford MK42 9AP
Tel 0234 228833/63222 ext 2833
County Archivist CJ Pickford

M–F 9.15–1 2–5
Photographs Microfilm Repair★
P M&T D (St Albans: parish records
of archdeaconry of Bedford)

Guide to the Bedfordshire Record Office,
1957, *Guide supplement 1957–62*, nd

BERKSHIRE

[5] **Berkshire Record Office**
Shire Hall, Shinfield Park, Reading
RG2 9XD
Tel 0734 875444 ext 3182
County Archivist JAS Green

● M 2–5, T–W 9–5, Th 9–9, F 9–4.30.
Closed two weeks in
October/November
Photographs Microfilm Repair★
P M&T D (Oxford: archdeaconry of
Berkshire)

F Hull, *Guide to the Berkshire Record Office*, 1952

[6] **Reading University Library**
PO Box 223, Whiteknights, Reading
RG6 2AE
Tel 0734 874331 ext 134/137
Keeper of Archives and Manuscripts
M Bott

● T–F 9–1 2–5
Photographs Microfilm Repair

JA Edwards, *Brief guide to archives
and manuscripts in the library,
University of Reading*, revised edn,
1983

[7] **Institute of Agricultural History
and Museum of English Rural Life**
University of Reading, PO Box 229,
Whiteknights, Reading RG6 2AG
Tel 0734 875123 ext 7677 and 475
Archivist DC Phillips

● M–T 9.30–1 2–5, F 9.30–1 2–4.30
Photographs Microfilm

*Guide to the Institute of Agricultural
History and Museum of English Rural
Life*, 1982

BUCKINGHAMSHIRE

[8] Buckinghamshire Record Office
County Hall, Aylesbury HP20 1UA
Tel 0296 395000 ext 587
County Archivist HA Hanley

● T-Th 9-5.15, F 9-4.45. Closed second week in February
Photographs Repair
P M&T D (Oxford: archdeaconry of Buckingham)

[9] Buckinghamshire Archaeological Society
County Museum, Church Street, Aylesbury HP20 2QP
Hon Archivist Mrs LM Head

W 10-4, or by arrangement
Photographs
M&T

CAMBRIDGESHIRE

[10] Cambridgeshire Record Office
Shire Hall, Cambridge CB3 0AP
Tel 0223 317281
County Archivist JM Farrar

M-Th 9-12.45 1.45-5.15 (● T to 9), F 9-12.45 1.45-4.15
Photographs Repair
P M&T D (Ely: parish records of archdeaconry of Ely and deaneries of Ely and March)

[11] Cambridgeshire Record Office
Grammar School Walk, Huntingdon PE18 6LF
Tel 0480 425842
Senior Archivist AD Hill

M-Th 9-12.45 1.45-5.15, F 9-12.45 1.45-4.15, ● second S in month 9-12
Photographs Repair
P M&T D (Ely: parish records of archdeaconry of Huntingdon)

GH Findlay, *Guide to the Huntingdonshire Record Office*, 1958

[12] Cambridge University Library
Department of Manuscripts, West Road, Cambridge CB3 9DR
Tel 0223 337733 ext 3143
Keeper of Manuscripts AEB Owen

M-F 9-6.45, S 9-12.30. Readers ticket. Closed one week in September
Photographs Microfilm Repair
P M&T D (Ely)

Catalogue of the manuscripts preserved in the library of the University of Cambridge, 6 vols, 1856-67. AEB Owen, *Summary guide to accessions of western manuscripts (other than medieval) since 1867*, 1966

Cambridge University Archives
Tel 0223 337733 ext 3149
Keeper of University Archives Mrs DM Owen
By appointment

HE Peek and CP Hall, *Archives of the University of Cambridge*, 1962

[13] Centre of South Asian Studies
Laundress Lane, Cambridge CB2 1SD
Tel 0223 338094
Secretary/Librarian LJ Carter

● M-F 9.30-5
Photographs

M Thatcher, *Cambridge South Asian Archive*, 3 vols, 1973-83

[14] Churchill Archives Centre
Churchill College, Cambridge CB3 0DS
Tel 0223 336087/336178
Keeper of the Archives CD Barnett
Archivist Ms E Bennett

● M-F 9-12.30 1.30-5
Photographs Repair

[15] Scott Polar Research Institute
Lensfield Road, Cambridge CB2 1ER
Tel 0223 336555
Archivist RK Headland

● M-F 10-12.30 2.30-5
Repair
P

C Holland, *Manuscripts in the Scott Polar Research Institute*, 1982

[16] **Trinity College Library**
Trinity College, Cambridge CB1 1TQ
Tel 0223 338488
Librarian DJ McKitterick

● M–F 9–5
Photographs

MR James, *The western manuscripts in the library of Trinity College, Cambridge*, 3 vols, 1900–2

CHESHIRE

[17] **Cheshire Record Office**
Duke Street, Chester CH1 1RL
Tel 0244 602574
County Archivist FI Dunn

● M–F 9.45–4.30
Repair*
P D (Chester. Liverpool: parish records of deaneries of Warrington and Farnworth)

[18] **Chester City Record Office**
Town Hall, Chester CH1 2HJ
Tel 0244 40144 ext 2108
City Archivist Miss AM Kennett

M–F 9–1 2–5 (● M to 9)
Repair*
P M&T

AM Kennett, *Archives and records of the City of Chester*, 1985

[19] **Warrington Library**
Museum Street, Warrington WA1 1JB
Tel 0925 571232
Principal Librarian D Rogers

M–W, F 9–7.30, Th, S 9–1
M&T

CLEVELAND

[20] **Cleveland County Archives Department**
Exchange House, 6 Marton Road, Middlesbrough TS1 1DB
Tel 0642 248321
County Archivist DH Tyrell

● M–Th 9–1 2–4.30, F 9–1 2–4
Photographs Repair
P D (York: Cleveland parish records)

CORNWALL

[21] **Cornwall Record Office**
County Hall, Truro TR1 3AY
Tel 0872 73698/74282 ext 3127
County Archivist Mrs CR North

● T–Th 9.30–1 2–5, F 9.30–1 2–4.30, S 9–12. Closed first two weeks in December
Photographs Microfilm Repair
P M&T D (Truro)

[22] **Royal Institution of Cornwall**
County Museum, River Street, Truro TR1 2SJ
Tel 0872 72205
Curator and Archivist HL Douch

M–S 9–1 2–5

CUMBRIA

[23] **Cumbria Record Office, Carlisle**
The Castle, Carlisle CA3 8UR
Tel 0228 23456 ext 2416
County Archivist Miss SJ MacPherson
Assistant County Archivist DM Bowcock

M–F 9–5
Photographs Microfilm Repair
P M&T D (Carlisle)

[24] **Cumbria Record Office, Kendal**
County Offices, Kendal LA9 4RQ
Tel 0539 21000 ext 329
County Archivist Miss SJ MacPherson
Assistant County Archivist JM Grisenthwaite

M–F 9–5
Photographs
P M&T D (Carlisle. Bradford: parish records)

[25] **Cumbria Record Office, Barrow**
140 Duke Street, Barrow-in-Furness
LA14 1XW
Tel 0229 31269
Area Archivist ACJ Jones

M–F 9–5
P M&T D (Carlisle: archdeaconry of Furness)

[29] **Exeter University Library**
Stocker Road, Exeter EX4 4PT
Tel 0392 263870
University Librarian JF Stirling

● M–S 9–5. Readers ticket required
Photographs Microfilm

Administrative assistance to Exeter Cathedral Library

Manuscript collections, 1976

DERBYSHIRE

[26] **Derbyshire Record Office**
County Offices, Matlock DE4 3AG
Tel 0629 3411 ext 7347
County Archivist Miss JC Sinar

● M–F 9.30–1 2–4.45
Photographs Repair*
P M&T D (Derby)

DORSET

[30] **Dorset Record Office**
County Hall, Dorchester DT1 1XJ
Tel 0305 204411 and 251000
County Archivist H Jaques

● M–F 9–1 2–5
Microfilm Repair
P M&T D (Salisbury: parish records of archdeaconries of Dorset and Sherborne)

DEVON

[27] **Devon Record Office**
Castle Street, Exeter EX4 3PU
Tel 0392 273509
County Archivist Mrs MM Rowe

M–Th 9.30–5, F 9.30–4.30, first and third S of month 9.30–12. Admission fee
Photographs Microfilm Repair*
P M&T D (Exeter)

From October 1987 will administer the dean and chapter archives in Exeter Cathedral Library

DURHAM

[31] **Durham County Record Office**
County Hall, Durham DH1 5UL
Tel 0385 64411 ext 2474/2253
County Archivist DJ Butler

● M, T, Th 8.45–4.45, W 8.45–8.30, F 8.45–4.15
Photographs Microfilm Repair*
P M&T D (Durham, Ripon: parish records)

WAL Seaman, *Durham County Record Office*, 1969

Local History Section, Darlington Library, Crown Street, Darlington DL1 1ND
Tel 0325 469858
Branch Archivist Mrs J Campbell

M–F 9–1 2–7, S 9–1 2–5

[28] **West Devon Record Office**
Unit 3, Clare Place, Coxside, Plymouth PL4 0JW
Tel 0752 264685
Senior Assistant Archivist Ms EA Stuart

M–Th 9.30–5 (to 7 on first W in month), F 9.30–4.30. Admission fee
D (Exeter: Plymouth archdeaconry)

[32] **Durham University Library**
Department of Special Collections, Palace Green, Durham DH1 3RN
Tel 0385 64466 ext 411/457
Keeper of Rare Books Miss EM Rainey

● M–F 9–5 (S 9–12.30 during term).
Readers ticket
Photographs Microfilm
M&T

D Ramage, *Summary list of additional manuscripts accessioned and listed between September 1945 and September 1961*, 1963

Oriental Section, Elvet Hill, Durham
DH1 3TH
Tel 0385 64971 ext 722/699
Keeper of Oriental Books Miss LE Forbes

● M–S 8.45–5 (term), M–S 9–1 2–5 (vacation)

[33] **Department of Palaeography and Diplomatic**
The Prior's Kitchen, The College, Durham DH1 3EQ
Tel 091-374 3615/6
5 The College, Durham DH1 3EQ
Tel 091-374 3610/1
Reader in Papyrology JD Thomas

M–F 10–1 2–5 (T to 8 during term).
Closed three weeks during summer
Microfilm Repair
P M&T D (Durham)

[34] **Durham Dean and Chapter Library**
The College, Durham DH1 3EH
Tel 091-386 2489
Deputy Chapter Librarian RC Norris

● M–F 10–1 2.15–5. Closed in August
Photographs Microfilm

RAB Mynors, *Durham cathedral manuscripts to the end of the twelfth century*, 1939

ESSEX

[35] **Essex Record Office**
County Hall, Chelmsford CM1 1LX
Tel 0245 267222 ext 2104
County Archivist VW Gray

● M 10–8.45, T–Th 9.15–5.15, F 9.15–4.15
Photographs Microfilm Repair*
P M&T D (Chelmsford)

FG Emmison, *Guide to the Essex Record Office*, 1969

[36] **Essex Record Office, Colchester and North-East Essex Branch**
Stanwell House, Stanwell Street, Colchester CO2 7DL
Tel 0206 572099
Branch Archivist PRJ Coverley

● M–Th 9.15–5.15, F 9.15–4.15
P D (Chelmsford: NE Essex parish records)

[37] **Essex Record Office, Southend Branch**
Central Library, Victoria Avenue, Southend-on-Sea SS2 6EX
Tel 0702 612621
Branch Archivist JR Smith

● M–Th 9.15–5, F 9.15–4.15
Photographs
M&T D (Chelmsford: SE Essex parish records)

GLOUCESTERSHIRE

[38] **Gloucestershire Record Office**
Clarence Row, off Alvin Street, Gloucester GL1 3DW
Tel 0452 425295
County and Diocesan Archivist DJH Smith

M–W, F 9–1, 2–5, Th 9–1 2–8.
Admission fee
Photographs Microfilm Repair
P M&T D (Gloucester)

Some classes of official records are available at the Shire Hall by appointment

A short handlist to the contents of the Gloucestershire Record Office, 1979

HAMPSHIRE

[39] Hampshire Record Office
20 Southgate Street, Winchester
SO 23 9EF
Tel 0962 63153
County Archivist Miss RC Dunhill

● M–Th 9–4.45, F 9–4.15, S 9.30–12
(second and fourth S only April–
September). Closed last full week
before Christmas
Photographs Microfilm Repair
P M&T D (Winchester)

[40] Portsmouth City Records Office
3 Museum Road, Portsmouth
PO1 2LE
Tel 0705 829765
City Records Officer Mrs SE Quail

M–W 9.30–12.30 2–5, Th 9.30–12.30
2–7, F 9.30–12.30 2–4
Photographs Microfilm Repair*
P M&T D (Portsmouth)

[41] Southampton City Record Office
Civic Centre, Southampton SO9 4XR
Tel 0703 832251/223855 ext 2251
City Archivist Miss SD Thomson

M–F 9–1, 1.30–5 and two evenings a
month to 9
Photographs Repair
P M&T D (Winchester: Southampton
parish records)

[42] Southampton University Library
Highfield, Southampton SO9 5NH
Tel 0703 559122 ext 3335/3724
Keeper of Special Collections G
Hampson
Archivist CM Woolgar

● M–F 9–1 2–5
Photographs Microfilm Repair

HEREFORD AND WORCESTER

[43] Hereford and Worcester Record Office
County Hall, Spetchley Road,
Worcester WR5 2NP
Tel 0905 353366 ext 3615
Head of Record Services AM Wherry

● M 10–4.45, T–Th 9.15–4.45,
F 9.15–4. Readers ticket
Microfilm
P D (Worcester)

[44] Hereford Record Office
The Old Barracks, Harold Street,
Hereford HR1 2QX
Tel 0432 265441
Assistant Head of Record Services
Miss DS Hubbard

M 10–1 2–4.45, T–Th 9.15–1 2–4.45,
F 9.15–1 2–4. Readers ticket
Microfilm Repair*
P M&T D (Hereford)

[45] Worcester (St Helen's) Record Office
Fish Street, Worcester WR1 2HW
Tel 0905 353366 ext 3616
Assistant Head of Record Services Mrs
E Howard

M 10–4.45, T–Th 9.15–4.45, F 9.15–4.
Readers ticket
Microfilm
P M&T D (Worcester)

HERTFORDSHIRE

[46] Hertfordshire Record Office
County Hall, Hertford SG13 8DE
Tel 0992 555105
County Archivist P Walne

M–Th 9.15–5.15, F 9.15–4.30
Photographs Repair
P M&T D (St Albans)

HUMBERSIDE

[47] Humberside County Record Office
County Hall, Beverley HU17 9BA
Tel 0482 867131 ext 3394
County Archivist KD Holt

● M, W, Th 9.15–4.45, T 9.15–8,
F 9.15–4. Closed last complete week in January
Photographs Microfilm Repair★
P M&T D (York: parish records of the archdeaconry of the East Riding)

[48] South Humberside Area Record Office
Town Hall Square, Grimsby DN31 1HX
Tel 0472 353481
Archivist in charge JF Wilson

● M–Th 9.30–12 1–5, F 9.30–12 1–4.15
Repair
P M&T

[49] Kingston upon Hull City Record Office
79 Lowgate, Hull HU1 2AA
Tel 0482 222015/6
Archivist GW Oxley

● M–Th 8.30–5, F 8.30–4.30
Photographs Repair
P M&T

[50] Hull University, Brynmor Jones Library
Cottingham Road, Hull HU6 7RX
Tel 0482 465265
Archivist N Higson (from October 1987 B Dyson)

● M–F 9–1 2–5
Photographs Microfilm
M&T

KENT

[51] Kent Archives Office
County Hall, Maidstone ME14 1XQ
Tel 0622 671411 ext 3363
County Archivist WN Yates

● T–F 9–4.30
Photographs Microfilm Repair★
P M&T D (Rochester. Canterbury: archdeaconry of Maidstone)

F Hull, *Guide to the Kent County Archives Office*, 1958, *First supplement*, 1971, *Second supplement*, 1983

West Kent Area Archives Office,
Central Library, The Drive, Sevenoaks
Tel 0732 452384
Archivist M Carter
By appointment

[52] Kent Archives Office, South East Kent Area
Central Library, Grace Hill, Folkestone CT20 1HD
Tel 0303 57583
Area Archivist Mrs MP Shaw

● M, Th 9–6, T, F 9–7, W 9–1, S 9–5
Photographs

Hythe Town Archives, Town Council Office, Oaklands, Stade Street, Hythe

● W 9.30–1 2–4.30

[53] Kent Archives Office, North East Kent Area
Ramsgate Library, Guildford Lawn, Ramsgate CT11 9A1
Tel 0843 593532 ext 3
Area Archivist Ms C Hodkin

● M–W, F 9.30–5.30, Th 9.30–5

[54] Canterbury Cathedral, City and Diocesan Record Office
The Precincts, Canterbury CT1 2EG
Tel 0227 463510
Archivist and Director Miss AM Oakley

● M–F 9.30–12.45 2–4.30. Closed third week in January, July and October and one week in April
Photographs Microfilm Repair
P M&T D (Canterbury)

LANCASHIRE

[55] Lancashire Record Office
Bow Lane, Preston PR1 8ND
Tel 0772 54868 ext 3039/3041
County Archivist K Hall

T 10–8.30, W–F 10–5. Readers ticket
Microfilm Repair
P M&T D (Blackburn. Bradford. Liverpool. Manchester)

RS France, *Guide to the Lancashire Record Office*, 3rd edn, 1985

LEICESTERSHIRE

[56] Leicestershire Record Office
57 New Walk, Leicester LE1 7JB
Tel 0533 544566
County Archivist Miss KM Thompson

M–Th 9.15–5, F 9.15–4.45, S 9.15–12.15. Readers ticket.
Closed first week in October
Photographs Microfilm Repair*
P M&T D (Leicester. Peterborough: Rutland parish records)

LINCOLNSHIRE

[57] Lincolnshire Archives Office
The Castle, Lincoln LN1 3AB
Tel 0522 25158
Principal Archivist GA Knight

M–F 9.15–4.45
Photographs Microfilm Repair*
P M&T D (Lincoln)

GREATER LONDON

[58] British Library, Department of Western Manuscripts
Great Russell Street, London WC1B 3DG
Tel 01–636 1544 ext 7508
Director of Special Collections Mrs S Tyacke

M–F 10–4.45. Readers ticket. Closed one week in November
Photographs Microfilm Repair*
P M&T

MAE Nickson, *The British Library: guide to the catalogues and indexes of the Department of Manuscripts*, 1978. *Catalogue of additions 1946–1950*, 3 vols, 1979. *Catalogue of additions 1951–1955*, 3 vols, 1982. *Index of MSS in the British Library*, 10 vols, 1984–1986

[59] British Library, India Office Library and Records
197 Blackfriars Road, London SE1 8NG
Tel 01–928 9531 ext 242
Director BC Bloomfield
Deputy Archivist MI Moir

M–F 9.30–6, S 9.30–1. Readers ticket
Photographs Microfilm Repair
P

W Foster, *A guide to the India Office records 1600–1858*, 1919 reprinted 1966

[60] British Museum (Natural History)
Cromwell Road, London SW7 5BD
Tel 01–589 6323 ext 671/238
Acting Museum Archivist Miss DM Norman

● M–F 10–4. Readers ticket
Photographs
P

Catalogue of the books, manuscripts, maps and drawings in the British Museum (Natural History), 5 vols and 3 supplementary vols, 1903–40. FC Sawyer, *A short history of the libraries and list of manuscripts and original drawings in the British Museum (Natural History)*, 1971

[61] House of Lords Record Office
House of Lords, London SW1A 0PW
Tel 01–219 3074
Clerk of the Records HS Cobb

● M–F 9.30–5. Closed last two weeks in November
Photographs Microfilm Repair

MF Bond, *Guide to the records of Parliament*, 1971

[62] **Imperial War Museum, Department of Documents**
Lambeth Road, London SE1 6HZ
Tel 01-735 8922
Keeper of the Department of Documents RWA Suddaby

M-F 10-5. Closed last two full weeks in October
Photographs Microfilm
P

[63] **National Army Museum, Department of Records**
Royal Hospital Road, London SW3 4HT
Tel 01-730 0717 ext 47
Deputy Director and Keeper of Records B Mollo

T-S 10-4.30. Readers ticket
Photographs Microfilm Repair

[64] **National Maritime Museum, Manuscripts Section**
Greenwich, London SE10 9NF
Tel 01-858 4422
Head of Manuscripts Section RA Morriss

M-F 10-5, S 10-1 2-5. Readers ticket. Closed on week in February
Photographs Microfilm Repair
P

RJB Knight, *Guide to the manuscripts in the National Maritime Museum*, 2 vols, 1977, 1980

[65] **Public Record Office**
Ruskin Avenue, Kew, Richmond TW9 4DU
Tel 01-876 3444
Chancery Lane, London WC2A 1LR
Tel 01-405 0741
Keeper of the Public Records GH Martin

M-F 9.30-5. Readers ticket. Closed first two weeks in October
Photographs Microfilm Repair*

Guide to the contents of the Public Record Office, 3 vols, 1963, 1968

The records now remaining at Chancery Lane comprise all those described in Vol 1 of the *Guide* (except the Copyright Office), those of some other legal departments etc with quasi-legal or related functions, the records of the State Paper Office, the Probate records and some gifts and deposits. The search room for census records is in Portugal Street, London WC2 (Tel 01-405 3488 ext 335)

[66] **Royal Air Force Museum, Department of Aviation Records (Archives)**
Aerodrome Road, Hendon, London NW9 5LL
Tel 01-205 2266 ext 210/211
Keeper of Aviation Records PG Murton

● M-F 10-5
Photographs Microfilm
P

[67] **Royal Botanic Gardens Library**
Kew, Richmond TW9 3AE
Tel 01-940 1171 ext 4417/4414
Chief Librarian and Archivist Miss SMD FitzGerald

● M-F 9-5. Readers ticket
Photographs
P

[68] **Science Museum Library**
South Kensington, London SW7 5NH
Tel 01-589 3456 ext 527
Assistant Keeper, Pictorial and Archives Collection DJ Bryden

● M-S 10-5.30. Readers ticket. Closed second week in July
Photographs Microfilm
P

[69] **Tate Gallery Archive**
Millbank, London SW1P 4RG
Tel 01-821 1313 ext 201/322
Head of Archives Miss SML Fox Pitt

● Th, F 10-1 2-5.30
Photographs Repair
P

[70] **Victoria & Albert Museum, National Art Library**
Cromwell Road, London SW7 2RL
Tel 01–589 6371 ext 331
Assistant Keeper, Special Collections
R Watson

M–Th 10–5, S 10–1 2–5. Readers ticket
Photographs Repair
P

Archive of Art & Design,
23 Blythe Road, London W14 0QF
Tel 01–603 1514
Curator in Charge Ms MM Sweet

● T–Th 10–1 2–4.30. Readers ticket

R Howell, *A guide to the Archive of Art & Design*, 1986

[71] **Greater London Record Office**
40 Northampton Road, EC1R 0HB
Tel 01–633 6851
Head Archivist Miss J Coburn

T–F 10–4.45 (T to 7.30 by appointment). Closed last two weeks in October
P M&T D (London, Southwark, Guildford)

[72] **Corporation of London Records Office**
PO Box 270, Guildhall, London EC2P 2EJ
Tel 01–606 3030 ext 1251
Deputy Keeper of the Records JR Sewell

M–F 9.30–4.45
P M&T

PE Jones and R Smith *Guide to the records at Guildhall London, part 1 the Corporation of London Records Office*, 1951

[73] **Guildhall Library**
Aldermanbury, London EC2P 2EJ
Tel 01–606 3030 ext 1863
Keeper of Manuscripts SGH Freeth

M–S 9.30–4.45
Photographs Microfilm Repair
P M&T D (London)

PE Jones and R Smith, *Guide to the records at Guildhall London, part II the Guildhall Library Muniment Room*, 1951

[74] **Barnet Local History Library**
Ravensfield House, The Burroughs,
London NW4 4BE
Tel 01–202 5625 ext 55
Borough Archivists Mrs JM Corden and Ms PJ Taylor

● M, Th, F 9.15–12.15, T, W 9.15–5, S 9–4
Photographs
M&T

[75] **Bexley Libraries and Museums Department**
Local Studies Section, Hall Place,
Bourne Road, Bexley DA5 1PQ
Tel 0322 526574 ext 217 and 218
Local Studies Officer/Archivist MD Barr-Hamilton

M–S 9–5
D (Rochester: parish records of deaneries of Erith and Sidcup)

[76] **Brent Leisure Services**
Grange Museum of Local History,
Neasden Lane, London NW10 1QB
Tel 01–908 7432
Local History Librarian/Archivist Ms PJ Campion

● M, T, Th, F 12–5, W 12–8, S 10–5

[77] **Bromley Public Libraries, Archives Section**
Central Library, High Street, Bromley BR1 1EX
Tel 01–460 9955 ext 261
Archivist Miss E Silverthorne

● T, Th 9.30–8, W, F 9.30–6, S 9.30–5 .
P D (Rochester: parish records of deaneries of Beckenham, Bromley and Orpington)

[78] **Camden Public Libraries**
Local History Library, Swiss Cottage
Library, 88 Avenue Road, London
NW3 3HA
Tel 01-586 5989 ext 234
Local History Librarian MJ Holmes

M-Th 9.30-8, F 9.30-6, S 9.30-5
Photographs Microfilm Repair

Local History Library, Holborn
Library, 32-38 Theobalds Road,
London WC1X 8PA
Tel 01-405 2706 ext 337
Deputy Local History Librarian
R Knight

● M, W 9-8, T, S 9-5, F 9-6

[79] **Greenwich Local History Library**
Woodlands, 90 Mycenae Road,
Blackheath, London SE3 7SE
Tel 01-858 4631
Local History Librarian J Watson

● M, T, Th 9-8, S 9-5
Photographs
P D (Southwark: Greenwich parish records)

[80] **Hackney Archives Department**
Rose Lipman Library, De Beauvoir
Road, London, N1 5SQ
Tel 01-241 2886
Archivist DL Mander

● M 2-8, T, Th, F 9.30-5, S 9.30-1 2-5
Photographs Repair*

[81] **Hammersmith and Fulham Archives**
Shepherd's Bush Library, 7 Uxbridge
Road, London W12 8LJ
Tel 01-743 0910, 01-748 3020 ext 3850
Borough Archivist C Jeans

● M, T, Th, F 9.30-5 (T to 9 by arrangement)
Photographs Repair

[82] **Haringey Libraries, Museum and Arts Department**
Bruce Castle Museum, Lordship Lane,
London N17 8NU
Tel 01-808 8772
Archivist IG Murray

● M-S 1-4.45
Photographs Microfilm
M&T

[83] **Kensington and Chelsea Libraries and Arts Service**
Central Library, Phillimore Walk,
London W8 7RX
Tel 01-937 2542 ext 3038 and 3004
Local Studies Librarian B Curle

● M, T, Th, F 10-8, W 10-1, S 10-5
Photographs

[84] **Lambeth Archives Department**
Minet Library, 52 Knatchbull Road,
London SE5 9QY
Tel 01-733 3279
Borough Archivists Mrs P Hatfield
and JA Newman

● M, T, Th, F 9.30-1 2-5, alternate
S 9.30-1 2-5
Repair
P M&T

MY Williams, *A short guide to the Surrey collection*, 1965

[85] **Lewisham Local History Centre**
The Manor House, Old Road, London
SE13 5SY
Tel 01-852 5050
Archivist CW Harrison

M, F, S 9.30-5, T, Th 9.30-8
Photographs
P M&T D (Southwark: parish records
of deaneries of East and West
Lewisham)

[86] **Redbridge Central Library**
Local History Room, Clements Road,
Ilford EG1 1EA
Tel 01-478 7145
Local History Librarian P Jackson

● T-F 9.30-8, S 9.30-4
Photographs

[87] **Southwark Local Studies Library**
211 Borough High Street, London
SE1 1JA
Tel 01-403 3507
Local Studies Librarian Miss NL Smith

● M, Th 9.30–12.30 1.30–8, T, F, 9.30–12.30 1.30–5, S 9.30–1

[88] **Tower Hamlets Libraries**
Local History Library, 277 Bancroft Road, London E1 4DQ
Tel 01-980 4366 ext 47
Archivist JJ Farrell

● M, T, Th, F 9–8, S 9–5
Photographs

[89] **Waltham Forest Archives**
Vestry House Museum, Vestry Road, Walthamstow, London E17 9NH
Tel 01-509 1917, 01-527 5544 ext 4391
Archivist RJ Evans

● T–F 10.30–1 2–5.30, S 10.30–1 2–5
M&T D (Chelmsford: parish records of deanery of Waltham Forest)

[90] **Westminster City Libraries, Archives Section**
Victoria Library, 160 Buckingham Palace Road, London SW1W 9UD
Tel 01-798 2180
Chief Archivist Miss MJ Swarbrick

M–F 9.30–7, S 9.30–1 2–5
P M&T D (London: Westminster parish records)

Local History Library, Marylebone Library, Marylebone Road, London NW1 5PS
Tel 01-798 1030
Archivist RA Bowden

● M–F 9.30–7, S 9.30–1 2–5
P

[91] **University of London Library**
Senate House, Malet Street, London WC1 7HU
Tel 01-636 4514 ext 5030
Archivist S Bailey

● M–F 9.30–5.30. Readers ticket. Closed one week in July
Photographs Microfilm Repair
M&T

RA Rye, *Catalogue of the manuscripts and autograph letters in the University Library ...*, 1921, Supplement 1921–30, 1930. *Catalogue of the Goldsmiths' Library of Economic Literature*, vol iii and iv 1982, 1983. J Percival, *A Guide to Archives and Manuscripts in the University of London*, vol 1, 1984

[92] **British Library of Political and Economic Science**
10 Portugal Street, London WC2A 2HD
Tel 01-405 7686 ext 2968
Archivist Angela Raspin

M–F 10–5.30 (vacation 10–5). Readers ticket. Closed one week at Easter, Christmas and in the summer
Photographs Microfilm

J Percival, *op cit*

[93] **Imperial College Archives**
Room 455, Sherfield Building, Imperial College, London SW7 2AZ
Tel 01-589 5111 ext 3021/2
College Librarian Mrs M Czigány

● M–F 10–5.30
Photographs

J Percival, *op cit*

[94] **Institute of Commonwealth Studies**
27–28 Russell Square, London WC1B 5DS
Tel 01-580 5876
Senior Assistant Librarian Miss SE Joynes

● M–W 10–7, Th–F 10–6 (term), M–F 10–5.30 (vacation)

[95] **King's College London, Liddell Hart Centre for Military Archives**
Strand, London WC2R 2LS
Tel 01-836 5454 ext 2187
College Archivist and Archivist to the Liddell Hart Centre
Miss PJ Methven

● M–F 9.30–5.30 (term), 9.30–4.30 (vacation). Closed last two weeks in August
Photographs Microfilm
P

Administers the College archives and manuscript collections

Liddell Hart Centre for Military Archives consolidated list of accessions, 1986. J Percival, *op cit*

[96] **School of Oriental and African Studies Library**
Malet Street, London WC1E 7HP
Tel 01-263 6013 ext 312
Archivist Mrs RE Seton

M–Th 9–8, F 9–6.30 (term), M–F 9–5 (vacation), S 9.30–12.30
Photographs Microfilm

Library Guide, 1980 (new edition in preparation). J Percival, *op cit*

[97] **University College London, Manuscripts Room**
The Library, Gower Street, London WC1E 6BT
Tel 01-387 7050 ext 2617/8
Archivist Ms GM Furlong

● M, W, Th 10–5.30, T 10–8, F 10–5 (term), M–F 10–5 (vacation). Readers ticket
Photographs Microfilm

DK Coveney, *Descriptive catalogue of manuscripts in the library of University College London*, 1935. *Manuscript collections in the library, a handlist*, typescript, 1978. J Percival, *op cit*

[98] **City of London Polytechnic, Fawcett Library**
Old Castle Street, London E1 7NT
Tel 01-283 1030 ext 570
Fawcett Librarian Miss CM Ireland

M–T 10–8.30, Th–F 10–5 (term), M–F 10–5 (vacation). Admission fee
Photographs Microfilm

[99] **British Architectural Library**
Royal Institute of British Architects, Manuscripts and Archives Collection, 66 Portland Place, London W1N 4AD
Tel 01-580 5533 ext 4321
Archivist Mrs A Mace

M 10–5, T–Th 10–8, F 10–7, S 10–1.30. Closed in August
Photographs Microfilm Repair

A Mace, *The Royal Institute of British Architects: a guide to its archive and history*, 1986.

Drawings Collection, 21 Portman Square, London W1H 9HP
Tel 01-580 5533 ext 4801
Curator of Drawings

● M–F 10–1. Closed in August

J Lever, *Catalogue of the drawings collection...*, 21 vols, 1968–81

[100] **Institution of Civil Engineers**
1–7 Great George Street, London SW1P 3AA
Tel 01-222 7722 ext 232
Archivist WA Morris

● M–F 9.15–5.30
Photographs

[101] **Institution of Electrical Engineers, Archives Department**
Savoy Place, London WC2R 0BL
Tel 01-240 1871 ext 336/290
Archivist Mrs EDP Symons

● M–F 10–5

[102] **Lambeth Palace Library**
London SE1 7JU
Tel 01-928 6222
Librarian EGW Bill

M–F 10–5
Repair
P M&T

HJ Todd, *Catalogue of the archiepiscopal manuscripts . . .*, 1812, continued by EGW Bill, *Catalogue of manuscripts . . .*, 3 vols, 1972, 1976, 1983

[103] **Linnean Society of London**
Burlington House, Piccadilly, London
W1V 0LQ
Tel 01-434 4479/4470
Librarian and Archivist Miss G Douglas

● M–F 10–5

Catalogue of the manuscripts in the library of the Linnean Society of London, parts 1–4, 1934–48

[104] **Royal Astronomical Society Library**
Burlington House, Piccadilly, London
W1V 0NL
Tel 01-734 4582/3307
Librarian PD Hingley

● M–F 10–5

JA Bennett, *Catalogue of the archives and manuscripts . . .*, 1978

[105] **Royal College of Physicians of London**
11 St Andrews Place, London
NW1 4LE
Tel 01-935 1174
Librarian G Davenport

M–F 9.30–5.30
P

[106] **Royal College of Surgeons of England**
35–43 Lincoln's Inn Fields, London
WC2A 3PN
Tel 01-405 3474 ext 8
Librarian IF Lyle

● M–F 10–6. Closed in August
Photographs
P

[107] **Royal Commonwealth Society Library**
18 Northumberland Avenue, London
WC2N 5BJ
Tel 01-930 6733
Librarian DH Simpson

● M–F 10–5.30. Readers ticket

DH Simpson, *The manuscript catalogue of the library . . .*, 1975

[108] **Royal Institution of Great Britain**
21 Albemarle Street, London
W1X 4BS
Tel 01-409 2992 ext 4
Librarian/Archivist Mrs IM McCabe

● M–F 10–5.30
Photographs Microfilm
P

[109] **Royal Society**
6 Carlton House Terrace, London
SW1Y 5AG
Tel: 01-839 5561 ext 259 and 260
Librarian NH Robinson

● M–F 10–5
Microfilm

RK Bluhm, 'A guide to the archives of the Royal Society and to other manuscripts in its possession', *Notes and records of the Royal Society of London* XII, 1956–57

[110] **Society of Antiquaries of London**
Burlington House, Piccadilly, London
W1V 0HS
Tel 01-734 0193, 01-437 9954
Librarian EB Nurse

● M–F 10–5

[111] **Society of Friends' Library**
Friends House, Euston Road, London
NW1 2BJ
Tel 01-387 3601
Librarian MJ Thomas

● T–F 10–5. Closed week preceding Spring Bank holiday and one week in August

[112] **Wellcome Institute for the History of Medicine**
183 Euston Road, London NW1 2BP
Tel 01-387 4477
Curator of Western Manuscripts RJ Palmer

M–F 9.45–5.15. Readers ticket
Photographs Microfilm Repair

SAJ Moorat, *Catalogue of western manuscripts on medicine and science in the Wellcome Historical Medical Library*, 3 vols, 1962, 1973. WR Dawson, *Manuscripta medica, a descriptive catalogue of the manuscripts in the Library of the Medical Society of London*, 1932

Contemporary Medical Archives Centre
Archivist Miss JGA Sheppard

● M–F 9.45–5.15. Readers ticket

Consolidated accessions list, 1985

[113] **Westminster Abbey Muniment Room and Library**
London SW1P 3PA
Tel 01-222 5152 ext 228
Keeper of the Muniments R Mortimer

● M–F 10–1 2–4.45
Photographs Repair
P

[114] **Westminster Diocesan Archives**
Archbishop's House, Ambrosden Avenue, London SW1P 1QJ
Tel 01-834 4717
Archivist Miss ER Poyser

● M–F 10–1 2–5

[115] **Dr Williams's Library**
14 Gordon Square, London WC1H 0AG
Tel 01-387 3727
Librarian JO Creasey

M, W, F 10–5, T, Th 10–6.30. Closed first two weeks of August

K Twinn, *Guide to the manuscripts . . .*, 1969. *Nonconformist congregations in Great Britian, a list of histories and other material in Dr Williams's Library*, 1973

GREATER MANCHESTER

[116] **Greater Manchester County Record Office**
56 Marshall Street, New Cross, Manchester M4 5FU
Tel 061-247 3383
County Archivist Miss M Patch

M, F 9–5, T–Th 9–6, ● second and fourth S of month
Photographs Microfilm Repair
P

CA Wright, *Summary of collections*, 1985

[117] **Bolton Archive Service**
Central Library, Civic Centre, Le Mans Crescent, Bolton BL1 1SE
Tel 0204 22311 ext 2179
Borough Archivist TK Campbell

● M, F 9.30–12 1–4.30, T 9.30–12.30, Th 1–7
Photographs
P

[118] **Bury Archive Service**
112 The Rock, Bury BL9 0PD
Tel 061-764 8625
Archivist KJ Mulley

● W 1–7.30 and by arrangement

Address correspondence to: Bury Libraries and Arts Department, Textile Hall, Manchester Road, Bury BL9 0DR

[119] **Manchester Central Library Archives Department**
St Peter's Square, Manchester M2 5PD
Tel 061-236 9422 ext 269
Archivist Miss JM Ayton

● M 9–12 1–9, T–F 9–12 1–5
Photographs Microfilm, Repair
P M&T D (Manchester)

15

[120] **Rochdale Libraries, Local Studies Department**
Area Central Library, Esplanade, Rochdale OL16 1AQ
Tel 0706 47474 ext 423
Local Studies and Archives Librarian J Cole

M, T, Th, 9.30–7.30, W 9.30–5, F 9.30–5.30, S 9.30–4
Photographs Microfilm

[121] **Salford Archives Centre**
658/662 Liverpool Road, Irlam, Manchester M30 5AD
Tel 061–775 5643
City Archivist AN Cross

● M–F 9–4.30
P

[122] **Stockport Archive Service**
Central Library, Wellington Road South, Stockport SK1 3RS
Tel 061–480 7297/3038
Archivist Mrs MJ Myerscough

● M–F 9–8, S 9–12
Photographs
P

MJ Critchlow, *Guide to archive calendars 1–14*, 1982

[123] **Tameside Local Studies Library**
Stalybridge Library, Trinity Street, Stalybridge SK15 2BN
Tel 061–338 2708/3831
Archivist Ms MW Chandley

M–W, F 9–7.30, S 9–4
Photographs
P

[124] **Wigan Record Office**
Town Hall, Leigh WN7 2DY
Tel 0942 672421 ext 266
Archivist AD Gillies

● M–F 10–4
Photographs Microfilm Repair*
P M&T D (Liverpool: parish records of archdeaconry of Wigan)

[125] **John Rylands University Library of Manchester**
Deansgate, Manchester M3 3EH
Tel 061–834 5343
Keeper of Manuscripts Miss GA Matheson

● M–F 10–5.30, S 10–1. Readers ticket
Photographs Microfilm Repair
M&T

Methodist Archives and Research Centre
Keeper of Printed Books DW Riley

● M–F 10–5.30, S 10–1

MERSEYSIDE

[126] **National Museums and Galleries on Merseyside**
Archives Department, 64–66 Islington, Liverpool L3 8LG
Tel 051–207 3697/8
Keeper of Archives J Gordon Read

● M, T, Th, F 9–5, W 10–5
Photographs
P

Martime Records Centre, Merseyside Maritime Museum, Pier Head, Liverpool L3 1DN
Tel 051–709 1551 ext 218
Assistant Keeper of Maritime Records Ms K Grant

M–F 10.30–4. Admission fee
Photographs

[127] **Liverpool Record Office and Local History Department**
City Libraries, William Brown Street, Liverpool L3 8EW
Tel 051–207 2147 ext 34
Local Studies and Archives Officer Miss J Smith

M–F 9–9, S 9–5
Photographs Microfilm Repair
P M&T D (Liverpool)

[128] **St Helens Local History and Archives Library**
Central Library, Gamble Institute, Victoria Square, St Helens WA10 1DY
Tel 0744 24061 ext 2952
Local History and Archives Librarian Mrs VL Hainsworth

● M–F 9–5, S 9–1, evenings by arrangement
Photographs Microfilm

[129] **Wirral Archives Service**
Birkenhead Reference Library, Borough Road, Birkenhead L41 2XB
Tel 051–652 6106/7/8 ext 34
Archivist DN Thompson

● M, T, Th, F 10–8, S 10–1 2–5
Photographs
P

[130] **Liverpool University, Sydney Jones Library**
PO Box 123, Liverpool L69 3DA
Tel 051–709 6022 ext 3126
Librarian VE Knight
Curator of Special Collections MR Perkin

● M–F 9–12 1–5

A guide to the manuscript collections in Liverpool University Library, 1962

[131] **Liverpool University Archives Unit**
PO Box 147, Liverpool L69 3BX
Tel 051–709 6022 ext 2315
University Archivist MG Cook

● M–F 9.30–5
Photographs

WEST MIDLANDS

[132] **Birmingham Central Libraries, Archives Department**
Chamberlain Square, Birmingham B3 3HQ
Tel 021–235 4217
Principal Archivist JD Davies

M–F 9–6, S 9–5
Photographs Microfilm Repair
P M&T D (Birmingham)

[133] **Coventry City Record Office**
Mandela House, Bayley Lane, Coventry CV1 5RG
Tel 0203 25555 ext 2768
City Archivist DJ Rimmer

● M–Th 8.45–4.45, F 8.45–4.15
Photographs Repair
P

[134] **Dudley Archives and Local History Department**
Dudley Library, St James's Road, Dudley DY9 9EL
Tel 0384 55433 ext 5514 and 5526
Archivist Mrs KH Atkins

● M, W, F 9–1 2–5, T, Th 2–7 first and third S in month 9.30–12.30
Photographs
P M&T D (Lichfield, Worcester: Dudley parish records)

[135] **Walsall Archives Service**
Local History Centre, Essex Street, Walsall WS2 7AS
Tel 0922 37305/6
Archivist/Local Studies Officer Mrs M Lewis

T, Th, F 9.30–5.30, W 9.30–7, S 9.30–1
Photographs Repair
P

[136] **Wolverhampton Borough Archives**
Central Library, Snow Hill, Wolverhampton WV1 3AX
Tel 0902 312025 ext 37
Borough Archivist Miss EA Rees

M–S 10–1 2–5
Photographs Repair
P

Bilston Branch Library, Mount Pleasant, Bilston WV14 7LU. By appointment

[137] **Birmingham University Library, Special Collections Department**
Main Library, PO Box 363, Birmingham B15 2TT
Tel 021–472 1301 ext 2439
Sub-Librarian (Special Collections) BS Benedikz

● M–F 9–5. Closed second week in July
Photographs Microfilm Repair★
P

Answers enquiries concerning Worcester dean and chapter records

[138] **Warwick University Modern Records Centre**
The University Library, Coventry CV4 7AL
Tel 0203 523523 ext 2014
Archivist RA Storey

M–Th 9–1 1.30–5, F 9–1 1.30–4. Closed one week at Easter and ten days at Christmas
Repair

RA Storey and A Tough, *Consolidated guide to the Modern Records Centre*, 1986

NORFOLK

[139] **Norfolk Record Office**
Central Library, Norwich NR2 1NJ
Tel 0603 611277 ext 262
County Archivist Miss JM Kennedy

● M–F 9–5, S 9–12
Photographs Microfilm Repair★
P M&T D (Norwich)

NORTHAMPTONSHIRE

[140] **Northamptonshire Record Office**
Delapré Abbey, London Road, Northampton NN4 9AW
Tel 0604 762129
Chief Archivist Miss R Watson

M–Th 9–4.45 (● Th to 7.45), F 9–4.30, ● two S each month 9–12.15
Photographs Microfilm Repair
P M&T D (Peterborough)

NORTHUMBERLAND

[141] **Northumberland Record Office**
Melton Park, North Gosforth, Newcastle upon Tyne NE3 5QX
Tel 091–236 2680
County Archivist RM Gard

M 9–9, T–Th 9–5, F 9–4.30
Photographs
P M&T D (Newcastle)

Berwick upon Tweed Record Office, Borough Council Offices, Wallace Green, Berwick upon Tweed

Th 10–1 2–5

NOTTINGHAMSHIRE

[142] **Nottinghamshire Record Office**
County House, High Pavement, Nottingham NG1 1HR
Tel 0602 504524
Principal Archivist AJM Henstock

M, W–F 9–4.45, T 9–7.15, S 9–12.15
Microfilm Repair★
P M&T D (Southwell)

PA Kennedy, *Guide to the Nottinghamshire County Records Office*, 1960

[143] **British Geological Survey Library**
Keyworth, Nottingham NG12 5GG
Tel 06077 6111 ext 3205
Chief Librarian and Archivist G McKenna

● M–F 9–4.30
Photographs

[144] **Nottingham University Library, Manuscripts Department**
University Park, Nottingham
NG7 2RD
Tel 0602 506101 ext 3440
Keeper of the Manuscripts Miss DB Johnston

● M–F 9–5
Photographs Microfilm Repair*
P M&T

OXFORDSHIRE

[145] **Oxfordshire County Record Office**
County Hall, New Road, Oxford
OX1 1ND
Tel 0865 815203
County Archivist Miss SJ Barnes

● M–Th 9–1 2–5, F 9–1 2–4
P M&T D (Oxford)

Oxfordshire County Record Office and its records, 1938. *Summary catalogue of the privately-deposited records in the Oxfordshire County Record Office*, 1966

[146] **Bodleian Library**
Department of Western Manuscripts, Bodleian Library, Oxford OX1 3BG
Tel 0865 277000 ext 286
Keeper of Western Manuscripts Mrs M Clapinson

M–F 9–10 (term), 9–7 (vacation), S 9–1. Readers ticket. Admission fee
Photographs Microfilm Repair
P M&T

F Madan and others, *Summary catalogue of western manuscripts in the Bodleian Library . . .*, 7 vols, 1895–1953, reprinted 1980

Administrative assistance to Oxford University Archives

Rhodes House Library, South Parks Road, Oxford OX1 3RG
Tel 0865 270909
Librarian AS Bell

● M–F 9–7 (term), 9–5 (vacation), S 9–1. Readers ticket. Admission fee

LB Frewer and WS Burne, *Manuscript collections . . .*, 4 vols, 1968–78

[147] **Nuffield College Library**
Oxford OX1 1NF
Tel 0865 248014
Librarian Ms C Kennedy

● M–F 9.30–1 2–6, S 9.30–1. Closed in August

[148] **Pusey House Library**
Pusey House, 61 St Giles, Oxford
OX1 3LZ
Tel 0865 278415
Custodian Revd HR Smythe

● M–Th 8.30–12.30 1.30–5.30, F 8.30–12.30. Readers ticket. Closed during long vacation

[149] **St Antony's College, Middle East Centre**
Oxford OX2 6JS
Tel 0865 59651 ext 264
Archivist Ms GM Grant

● M–F 9.30–5.15. Closed two weeks at Easter and Christmas and for August
Photographs

D Grimwood-Jones, *Sources for the history of the British in the Middle East 1800–1978. A catalogue of the private papers collection . . .*, 1979

SHROPSHIRE

[150] **Shropshire Record Office**
Shirehall, Abbey Foregate, Shrewsbury
SY2 6ND
Tel 0743 252851/3
County Archivist Mrs MT Halford

● M, T, Th 9.30–12.40 1.20–5, F 9.30–12.40 1.20–4. Closed two weeks in late autumn
Repair
P M&T D (Hereford: parish records

of archdeaconry of Ludlow. Lichfield: archdeaconry of Salop)

MC Hill, *A guide to the Shropshire records*, 1952

[151] **Shropshire Libraries, Local Studies Department**
Castle Gates, Shrewsbury SY1 2AS
Tel 0743 61058
Local Studies Librarian AM Carr

M, W 9.30–12.30 1.30–5.30, T, F 9.30–12.30 1.30–7.30, S 9.30–12.30 1.30–5
Photographs
M&T D (Hereford: parish records of archdeaconry of Ludlow. Lichfield: parish records of archdeaconry of Salop)

SOMERSET

[152] **Somerset Record Office**
Obridge Road, Taunton TA2 7PU
Tel 0823 337600
County Archivist DMM Shorrocks

● M–Th 9–4.50, F 9–4.20, S 9.15–12.15
Repair*
P M&T D (Bath and Wells)

STAFFORDSHIRE

[153] **Staffordshire Record Office**
Eastgate Street, Stafford ST16 2LZ
Tel 0785 3121 ext 8380
County Archivist DV Fowkes

M–Th 9–1 1.30–5, F 9–1 1.30–4.30,
● S 9.30–1
Repair
P M&T D (Lichfield)

[154] **William Salt Library**
Eastgate Street, Stafford ST16 2LZ
Tel 0785 52276
Librarian DV Fowkes

T–Th 9–1 2–5, F 9–1 2–4.30, second and fourth S in month 9.30–1
M&T

[155] **Lichfield Joint Record Office**
Lichfield Library, Bird Street, Lichfield WS13 6PN
Tel 0543 256787
Archivist (historical enquiries) Mrs J Hampartumian
Principal Area Librarian (genealogical enquiries) Miss EM Hughes

● M, T, Th, F 10–5.15, W 10–4.30
P M&T D (Lichfield)

[156] **Keele University Library**
Keele ST5 5BG
Tel 0782 621111 ext 255
Archivist Mrs C Fyfe

● M–F 9.30–5, S 9.30–12. Closed ten days at Easter, August bank holiday and Christmas
Photographs Microfilm

SUFFOLK

[157] **Suffolk Record Office**
County Hall, Ipswich IP4 2JS
Tel 0473 230000 ext 4235,
0473 230732 Sat only
County Archivist Miss AJE Arrowsmith

M–Th 9–5, F 9–4, S 9–1 2–5
Photographs Microfilm Repair*
P M&T D (St Edmundsbury and Ipswich: archdeaconries of Ipswich and Suffolk)

[158] **Suffolk Record Office, Bury St Edmunds Branch**
Raingate Street, Bury St Edmunds IP33 1RX
Tel 0284 63141 ext 2522
Senior Assistant Archivist RG Thomas

M–Th 9–5, F 9–4, S 9–1 2–5
Photographs Microfilm Repair*
P M&T D (St Edmundsbury and Ipswich: archdeaconry of Sudbury)

[159] **Suffolk Record Office, Lowestoft Branch**
Central Library, Clapham Road, Lowestoft NR32 1DR
Tel 0502 66325 ext 274
Archivist in charge Miss RA Rogers

M–Th 9.15–5, F 9.15–6, S 9.15–5
P M&T D (St Edmundsbury and Ipswich: NE Suffolk parish records)

SURREY

[160] **Surrey Record Office**
County Hall, Penrhyn Road, Kingston upon Thames KT1 2DN
Tel 01–541 9065
County Archivist DB Robinson

M–W, F 9.30–4.45, ● second and fourth S of month 9.30–12.30
Repair
P M&T D (Southwark: parish records. Guildford: parish records of Emly and Epsom deaneries)

The records in Kingston upon Thames Muniment Room are made available in the searchroom, by appointment
Tel 01–541 9064
Borough Archivist Mrs A McCormack

Guide to the Kingston borough archives, 1971

[161] **Surrey Record Office, Guildford Muniment Room**
Castle Arch, Guildford GU1 3SX
Tel 0483 573942
Archivist in charge Mrs SF Corke

● T–Th 9.30–12.30 1.45–4.45, first and third S of month 9.30–12.30
P M&T D (Guildford)

Summary guide to Guildford Muniment Room, 1967

EAST SUSSEX

[162] **East Sussex Record Office**
The Maltings, Castle Precincts, Lewes BN7 1YT
Tel 0273 475400 ext 12 and 359
County Records Officer CR Davey

M–Th 8.45–4.45, F 8.45–4.15
Microfilm Repair
P D (Chichester: East Sussex parish records)

JA Brent, *East Sussex Record Office: a short guide*, 1983

[163] **Royal Greenwich Observatory**
Herstmonceux Castle, Hailsham BN27 1RP
Tel 0323 833171 ext 3379 and 3211
Librarian Archivist Miss J Dudley

● M–F 9–5.30, S and evenings by arrangement
Photographs Repair
P

[164] **Sussex University Library**
Falmer, Brighton BN1 9QL
Tel 0237 606755 ext 3492
Librarian Miss EM Rodger

● M–F 9–5.15
Photographs

WEST SUSSEX

[165] **West Sussex Record Office**
County Hall, Chichester PO19 1RN
Tel 0243 777983
County Archivist Mrs P Gill

M–F 9.15–12.30 1.30–5
Repair
P M&T D (Chichester)

TYNE AND WEAR

[166] **Tyne and Wear Archives Service**
Blandford House, West Blandford Street, Newcastle upon Tyne NE1 4JA
Tel 091–232 6789
Chief Archivist B Jackson

● M, W–F 8.45–5.15, T 8.45–8.30
Photographs Microfilm Repair*
P M&T

Local Studies Centre, Howard Street,
North Shields NE30 1LY
Tel 091-258 2811 ext 17

M, W–F 9–1 2–5, T 9–1 2–7

[167] **Gateshead Central Library, Local Studies Collection**
Prince Consort Road, Gateshead
NE8 4LN
Tel 091-447 3478
Local Studies Librarian TS Marshall

M, T, Th, F 9.30–7.30, W 9.30–5,
S 9.30–1
Photographs
P M&T

FWD Manders, *Gateshead archives: a guide*, 1968

[168] **Newcastle upon Tyne University Library**
Newcastle upon Tyne NE2 4HQ
Tel 091-232 8511 ext 3671 and 3656
Special Collections Librarians RS Firth and Miss L Gordon

● M–F 9.15–5
Microfilm Repair*

WARWICKSHIRE

[169] **Warwick County Record Office**
Priory Park, Cape Road, Warwick
CV34 4JS
Tel 0926 493431 ext 2508
County Archivist MW Farr

M–Th 9–1 2–5.30, F 9–1 2–5,
S 9–12.30. Readers ticket
Photographs Microfilm Repair
P M&T D (Coventry. Birmingham: parish records)

[170] **Shakespeare Birthplace Trust Records Office**
Henley Street, Stratford-upon-Avon
CV37 6QW
Tel 0789 204016
Senior Archivist R Bearman

M–F 9.30–1 2–5, S 9.30–12.30
Photographs
P M&T D (Coventry: Stratford-upon-Avon parish records)

ISLE OF WIGHT

[171] **Isle of Wight County Record Office**
26 Hillside, Newport PO30 2EB
Tel 0983 524031 ext 132/3
County Archivist CD Webster

M, T, Th, F 9.30–5, W 9.30–8.30
Photographs
P M&T D (Portsmouth: parish records of archdeaconry of Isle of Wight)

WILTSHIRE

[172] **Wiltshire Record Office**
County Hall, Trowbridge BA14 8JG
Tel 022-14 3641 ext 3502
County Archivist KH Rogers

M, T, Th, F 9–5, W 9–8.30
Photographs Microfilm Repair
P M&T D (Salisbury. Bristol: parish records of archdeaconry of Swindon)

NORTH YORKSHIRE

[173] **North Yorkshire County Record Office**
County Hall, Northallerton DL7 8AD
Tel 0609 3123 ext 2455
County Archivist MY Ashcroft

● M, T, Th, F 8.50–4.50, W 8.50–8.50
Microfilm Repair
P M&T D (Bradford, Ripon, York: parish records)

[174] **National Railway Museum Library**
Leeman Road, York YO2 4XJ
Tel 0904 21261
Keeper JA Coiley

● T–F 10.30–5. Readers ticket
Photographs

[175] **York City Archives Department**
Art Gallery Buildings, Exhibition Square, York YO1 2EW
Tel 0904 51533
City Archivist Mrs RJ Freedman

T–Th 9.30–12.30 2–5.30,
● M, F 9.30–12.30 2–5.30
Photographs Microfilm
P

[176] **York University, Borthwick Institute of Historical Research**
St Anthony's Hall, Peasholme Green, York YO1 2PW
Tel 0904 642315
Director DM Smith

● M–F 9.30–12.50 2–4.50. Closed two weeks at August bank holiday
Photographs Microfilm Repair*
P M&T D (York)

DM Smith, *A guide to the archive collections in the Borthwick Institute of Historical Research*, 1973, Supplement, 1980

[177] **York Minster Library**
Dean's Park, York YO1 2JD
Tel 0904 25308
Archivist Miss SG Beckley

● M–F 9–5

SOUTH YORKSHIRE

[178] **Barnsley Archive Service**
Central Library, Shambles Street, Barnsley S70 2JF
Tel 0226 283241 ext 23
Archivist Miss RF Vyse

M–W 9.30–1 2–6, F 9.30–1 2–5,
● S 9.30–1

[179] **Doncaster Archives Department**
King Edward Road, Balby, Doncaster DN4 0NA
Tel 0302 859811
Archivist B Barber

M–F 9.30–12.30 2–5
P D (Sheffield: archdeaconry of Doncaster)

Guide to the archives department, 1981

[180] **Rotherham Metropolitan Borough, Brian O'Malley Central Library**
Walker Place, Rotherham S65 1JH
Tel 0709 382121 ext 3583
Archivist AP Munford

M, T, F 10–5, W 1–7, Th 10–7, S 9–5
Photographs

[181] **Sheffield Record Office**
Central Library, Surrey Street, Sheffield S1 1XZ
Tel 0742 734756
Principal Archivist DA Postles

● M–F 9.30–5.30 (second M of month to 8.30), S 9–4.30
Photographs Microfilm Repair*
P M&T D (Sheffield)

Also houses the holdings of the former South Yorkshire County Record Office

R Meredith, *Guide to the manuscript collections in the Sheffield City Libraries*, 1956, Supplement (accessions 1956–76), 1976

[182] **Sheffield University Library**
Western Bank, Sheffield S10 2TN
Tel 0742 768555 ext 4333
Deputy Librarian W J Hitchens

● M–Th 9–9.30, F 9–5, S 9–1(term),
M–F 9–5, S 9–12.30 (vacation).
Readers ticket
Photographs Microfilm

WEST YORKSHIRE

[183] **West Yorkshire Archives, Headquarters and Wakefield**
Registry of Deeds, Newstead Road, Wakefield WF1 2DE
Tel 0924 367111 ext 2352
Archivist to the Joint Committee RL Frost

M 9–8, T–Th 9–5, F 9–1
Microfilm Repair*
P M&T D (Wakefield)

[184] **West Yorkshire Archives, Bradford**
15 Canal Road, Bradford BD1 4AT
Tel 0274 731931
District Archivist D James

● M–F 9.30–1 2–5
P D (Bradford)

[185] **West Yorkshire Archives, Calderdale**
Central Library, Northgate House, Northgate, Halifax HX1 1UN
Tel 0422 57257 ext 2636
District Archivist A Betteridge

M, T, Th, F 10–5.30, ● W 10–12
P D (Bradford: parish records)

Archives in Calderdale, 1976

[186] **West Yorkshire Archives, Kirklees**
Central Library, Princess Alexandra Walk, Huddersfield HD1 2SU
Tel 0484 513808 ext 207
District Archivist Miss J Burhouse

M–Th 9–8, F 9–4, ● S
P M&T

[187] **West Yorkshire Archives, Leeds**
Chapeltown Road, Sheepscar, Leeds LS7 3AP
Tel 0532 628339
District Archivist WJ Connor

● M–F 9.30–5
Microfilm Repair
P M&T D (Ripon. Bradford: parish records)

[188] **Leeds University, Brotherton Library**
Leeds LS2 9JT
Tel 0532 431751 ext 7278
University Librarian and Keeper of the Brotherton Collection RP Carr
Sub-Librarian, Special Collections PS Morrish

● M–F 9–5
Photographs Microfilm

Brotherton Collection
Tel 0532 431751 ext 6552
Sub-Librarian in charge CDW Sheppard

● M–F 9–1 2.15–5, S by arrangement

The Brotherton Collection, University of Leeds; its contents described . . ., 1986

[189] **Yorkshire Archaeological Society**
Claremont, 23 Clarendon Road, Leeds LS2 9NZ
Tel 0532 456362
Archivist in charge Mrs S Thomas

● M (unless open the previous S), Th, F 9.30–5, T, W 2–8.30, first and third S of month 9.30–5
Microfilm
M&T

EW Crossley, *Catalogue of manuscripts and deeds in the library of Yorkshire Archaeological Society*, 1931, reprinted 1986. S Thomas, *Guide to the archives of the Yorkshire Archaeological Society 1931–1983 and to collections deposited with the Society*, 1985

WALES

CLWYD

[190] Clwyd Record Office, Hawarden Branch
The Old Rectory, Hawarden, Deeside
CH5 3NR
Tel 0244 532364
County Archivist AG Veysey

● M–Th 9–4.45, F 9–4.15
Photographs Repair*
P M&T D (St Asaph: parish records)

Administrative assistance to St Deiniol's Library, Hawarden

AG Veysey, *Guide to the Flintshire Record Office*, 1974

[191] Clwyd Record Office, Ruthin Branch
46 Clwyd Street, Ruthin LL15 1HP
Tel 08242 3077
Senior Assistant Archivist RK Matthias

● M–Th 9–4.45, F 9–4.15
Photographs Repair*
P M&T D (St Asaph: parish records)

DYFED

[192] National Library of Wales, Department of Manuscripts and Records
Aberystwyth SY23 3BU
Tel 0970 3816
Keeper of Manuscripts and Records
D Huws

M–F 9.30–6, S 9.30–5. Readers ticket
Photographs Microfilm Repair
P M&T D (Province of Wales)

Catalogue of manuscripts, vol 1, 1921.
Handlist of manuscripts in the National Library of Wales, vols I–IV, 1940–86

[193] Dyfed Archive Service, Carmarthenshire Area Record Office
County Hall, Carmarthen SA31 1JP
Tel 0267 233333 ext 4184
County Archivist J Owen

M–Th 9–4.45, F 9–4.15, ● first and third S of month 9.30–12.30
P M&T D (St Davids: parish records)

S Beckley, *Carmarthenshire Record Office: a survey of archive holdings*, 1980

[194] Cardiganshire Area Record Office
County Office, Marine Terrace, Aberystwyth SY23 2DE
Tel 0970 617581 ext 2120
Records Assistant Janet Marx

T, Th 9–1 2–4.45
P M&T D (St Davids: parish records)

[195] Pembrokeshire Area Record Office
The Castle, Haverfordwest SA61 2EF
Tel 0437 3707
Archivist in charge C Hughes

M–Th 9–4.45, F 9–4.15, first and third S of month 9.30–12.30
Repair
P M&T D (St Davids: parish records)

SOUTH GLAMORGAN

[196] Glamorgan Archive Service
(for Mid, South and West Glamorgan)
Glamorgan Record Office, County Hall, Cathays Park, Cardiff CF1 3NE
Tel 0222 820282
Glamorgan Archivist Mrs P Moore

T–Th 9–5, F 9–4.30
Photographs Repair*
P M&T D (Llandaff, Swansea and Brecon: parish records)

WEST GLAMORGAN

[197] West Glamorgan Area Record Office
County Hall, Oystermouth Road,
Swansea SA1 3SN
Tel 0792 471589
Assistant Archivist in charge Mrs E Bennett

M–W 9–12.45 2–4.45 (● M 5.30–7.30)
P M&T D (Swansea and Brecon: parish records)

[198] University College of Swansea Library
Singleton, Swansea SA2 8PP
Tel 0792 205678 ext 4042
Archivist DA Bevan

● M–S 9–5, evenings until 10 by arrangement. Closed S in vacations
Photographs Microfilm

GWENT

[199] Gwent County Record Office
County Hall, Cwmbran NP44 2XH
Tel 06333 838838
County Archivist D Tibbott

T–Th 9.30–5, F 9.30–4
Photographs Microfilm Repair
P M&T D (Monmouth, Swansea and Brecon: parish records)

WH Baker, *Guide to the Monmouthshire Record Office*, 1959

GWYNEDD

[200] Gwynedd Archives and Museums Service, Caernarfon Area Record Office
Victoria Dock, Caernarfon
Tel 0286 4121 ext 2095
County Archivist and Museums Officer BR Parry
Deputy County Archivist G Haulfryn Williams

Address correspondence to County Offices, Caernarfon LL55 1SH

● M, T, Th, F 9.30–12.30 1.30–5,
W 9.30–12.30 1.30–7
Photographs Repair★
P M&T D (Bangor. St Asaph: parish records)

WO Williams, *Guide to the Caernarvonshire Record Office*, 1952

[201] Dolgellau Area Record Office
Cae Penarlag, Dolgellau LL40 2YB
Tel 0341 422341 ext 261
Area Archivist and Museums Officer Miss A Rhydderch

● M, T, Th, F 9–1 2–5 (Th to 7 by arrangement), W 9–1 2–7
Photographs Repair
P M&T

[202] Llangefni Area Record Office
Shire Hall, Llangefni LL77 7TW
Tel 0248 750262 ext 269
Area Archivist EW Thomas

M–F 9–1 2–5
P M&T D (Bangor: Anglesey parish records)

[203] University College of North Wales Library, Department of Manuscripts
Bangor LL57 2DG
Tel 0248 351151 ext 316
Archivist and Keeper of Manuscripts T Roberts

M–F 9–1 2–5 (W to 9 in term)
Photographs Repair★
P M&T

POWYS

[204] Powys Library Headquarters, Archives
Cefnllys Road, Llandrindod Wells LD1 5LD
Tel 0597 2212
Archivist R Morgan

● M–Th 9–5, F 9–4
P

SCOTLAND

CENTRAL

[205] **Central Regional Council Archives Department**
Old High School, Spittal Street, Stirling FK8 1DG
Tel 0786 73111 ext 466
Regional Archivist GA Dixon

M–F 9–5
Photographs
P(S)

DUMFRIES AND GALLOWAY

[206] **Dumfries and Galloway Regional Library Service**
Ewart Public Library, Catherine Street, Dumfries DG1 1JB
Tel 0387 53820
Reference and Local Collection Librarian ABG Cowper

● M–W, F 10–7.30, Th, S 10–5
P(S)

[207] **Dumfries Archive Centre**
33 Burns Street, Dumfries DG1 2PS
Tel 0387 69254
Archivist Miss MM Stewart

● T–F 2–5

FIFE

[208] **St Andrews University Library**
North Street, St Andrews KY16 9TR
Tel 0334 76161 ext 514
Keeper of Manuscripts RN Smart

M–F 9–1 2–5 (S 9–12 during term)
Photographs Microfilm Repair★
P(S)

GRAMPIAN

[209] **Grampian Regional Archives**
Old Aberdeen House, Dunbar Street, Aberdeen AB2 1UE
Tel 0224 481775
Regional Archivist Mrs BR Cluer

● M–F 9–5
Photographs

[210] **Moray District Record Office**
Tolbooth, High Street, Forres
IV36 0AB
Tel 0309 73617
District Archivist DA Iredale

M–F 9–12.30 1.30–4.30
Photographs Repair
P(S)

[211] **Aberdeen City Archives**
Town House, Aberdeen AB9 1AQ
Tel 0224 642121 ext 513
Archivist Miss JA Cripps

● M–F 9.30–12.30 2–4.30
Photographs

[212] **Aberdeen University Library, Department of Manuscripts and Archives**
King's College, Aberdeen AB9 2UB
Tel 0224 480241 ext 5112
Archivist and Keeper of Manuscripts CA McLaren

● M–F 9.15–4.30
Photographs Microfilm

HIGHLAND

[213] **Highland Regional Archive**
The Library, Farraline Park, Inverness
Tel 0463 236463
Records Officer AB Lawson

● M–F 9.30–5.30

LOTHIAN

[214] National Library of Scotland, Department of Manuscripts
George IV Bridge, Edinburgh
EH1 1EW
Tel 031–226 4531
Keepers of Manuscripts PM Cadell and TI Rae

M–F 9.30–8.30, S 9.30–1. Readers ticket
Photographs Microfilm Repair

Summary catalogue of the Advocates' manuscripts, 1971, *Catalogue of manuscripts acquired since 1925*, 6 vols, 1938–86

[215] Royal Botanic Garden
The Library, Inverleith Row, Edinburgh EH3 5LR
Tel 031–552 7171 ext 223
Librarian MV Mathew

● M–Th 8.30–1 2–5, F 8.30–1 2–4.30
Photographs

[216] Scottish Record Office
HM General Register House, Princes Street, Edinburgh EH1 3YY
Tel 031–556 6585
Keeper of the Records of Scotland AL Murray

West Register House, Charlotte Square, Edinburgh EH2 4DF
Tel 031–556 6585 ext 287
Deputy Keeper AM Broom

M–F 9–4.45. Readers ticket. HM General Register House closed first two weeks and West Register House third week of November
Microfilm Repair*

The National Register of Archives (Scotland) is maintained at West Register House

M Livingstone, *Guide to the public records of Scotland deposited in HM General Register House Edinburgh*, 1905. *List of gifts and deposits in the Scottish Record Office* vol 1, 1971, vol 2, 1976

[217] City of Edinburgh District Council Archives
Department of Administration, City Chambers, High Street, Edinburgh EH1 1YJ
Tel 031–225 2424 ext 5196
City Archivist AT Wilson

● M–Th 9.30–12.30 2–4.30,
F 9.30–12.30 2–3.45

[218] Edinburgh University Library, Special Collections Department
George Square, Edinburgh EH8 9LJ
Tel 031–667 1011 ext 6628
Librarian, Special Collections
J Howard

● M–F 9–5. Readers ticket. Closed second week in August
Photographs Microfilm Repair

Index to manuscripts, Edinburgh University Library, 2 vols, 1964, *First supplement*, 1981

New College Library (Faculty of Divinity), Mound Place, Edinburgh EH1 2LU
Tel 031–225 8400

● M–F 9–5. Readers ticket

[219] Scottish Catholic Archives
Columba House, 16 Drummond Place, Edinburgh EH3 6PL
Tel 031–556 3661
Keeper Revd GM Dilworth

● M–F 9.30–5.30

ORKNEY

[220] Orkney Archives
The Orkney Library, Laing Street, Kirkwall KW15 1NW
Tel 0856 3166 ext 5
Archivist Miss A Fraser

● M–F 9–1 2–5
Photographs
P(S)

SHETLAND

[221] Shetland Archives
44 King Harald Street, Lerwick
ZE1 0EQ
Tel 0595 3535 ext 269
Archivist BR Smith

● M–Th 9–1 2–5, F 9–1 2–4
Photographs
P(S)

STRATHCLYDE

[222] Strathclyde Regional Archives
Mitchell Library, North Street,
Glasgow G3 7DN
Tel 041–227 2401/5
Principal Archivist AM Jackson

M–Th 9.30–4.45, F 9.30–4
Photographs Repair*
P(S)

Ayrshire Subregional Archives,
County Buildings, Wellington Square,
Ayr

W 10–4
P(S)

[223] Argyll and Bute District Archives
Argyll and Bute District Council,
Kilmory, Lochgilphead PA31 8RT
Tel 0546 2127 ext 120
Archivist MIM MacDonald

M–Th 9–1 2–5.15, F 9–1 2–4
Microfilm

[224] City of Glasgow, Mitchell Library
201 North Street, Glasgow G3 7DN
Tel 041–221 7030 ext 171
Departmental Librarian, Rare Books
and Manuscripts Miss HM Wright

● M–F 9.30–9, S 9.30–5
Photographs Microfilm Repair
P(S)

[225] Glasgow University Library, Special Collections Department
Hillhead Street, Glasgow G12 8QE
Tel 041–339 8855 ext 6767
Keeper of Special Collections PK Escreet

M–F 9.15–9 (term), 9.15–4.45
(vacation), S 9.15–12.15 (term only).
Readers ticket required
Photographs Repair

J Young and PH Aitken, *A catalogue of the manuscripts in the Library of the Hunterian Museum . . .*, 1908

[226] Glasgow University Archives
The University, Glasgow G12 8QQ
Tel 041–339 8855 ext 5516/4543
University Archivist MS Moss

M–F 9–5, S and evenings in term by
arrangement. Readers ticket
Photographs Microfilm Repair
P(S)

Adam Smith Business Record Centre
Manager Mrs A Topen

● M–F 9–5

[227] Strathclyde University Archives
University of Strathclyde, Glasgow
G1 1XQ
Tel 041–552 4400 ext 2318
Archivist JS McGrath

● M–F 9–5
Photographs

[228] Royal College of Physicians and Surgeons of Glasgow
234–242 St Vincent Street, Glasgow
G2 5RJ
Tel 041–221 6072
Librarian AM Rodger

● M–F 9.30–5.30

TAYSIDE

[229] **Dundee District Archive and Record Centre**
City Chambers, City Square, Dundee DD1 3BY
Tel 0382 23141 ext 4494
Archivist IEF Flett

● M–F 9–1 2–5
P(S)

Acts on an agency basis for Tayside Region

[230] **Perth and Kinross District Archive**
Sandeman Library, 16 Kinnoull Street, Perth PH1 5ET
Tel 0738 23329
Archivist SJ Connelly

● M–F 9.30–1 2–5
P(S)

[231] **Perth Museum and Art Gallery**
George Street, Perth PH1 5LB
Tel 0738 32488
Keeper of Human History Ms S Payne

● M–F 10–1 2–5
Photographs

[232] **Dundee University Library, Archives and Manuscripts Department**
Dundee DD1 4HN
Tel 0382 23181 ext 4095
Archivist Mrs HJ Auld

● M–F 9–5
Photographs Repair

NORTHERN IRELAND

[233] **Public Record Office of Northern Ireland**
66 Balmoral Avenue, Belfast BT9 6NY
Tel 0232 661621/663286
Director B Trainor

M–F 9.15–4.45. Readers ticket. Closed first two weeks in December
Photographs Microfilm Repair

THE ISLE OF MAN

[234] **Manx Museum Library**
Kingswood Grove, Douglas
Tel 0624 75522/25125 ext 133
Librarian-Archivist Miss AM Harrison

M–F 10–5
Repair
D (Sodor and Man)

Register Offices

[235] **Office of Population Censuses and Surveys**
St Catherine's House, 10 Kingsway, London WC2B 6JP
Tel 01-242 0262 ext 2446
Director and Registrar General AR Thatcher

M-F 8.30-4.30

Has custody of all statutory registers of births, marriages and deaths in England and Wales since 1837

[236] **Principal Registry of the Family Division**
Somerset House, Strand, London WC2R 1LP
Tel 01-936 6960
Senior Registrar BP Tickle

M-F 10-4.30

Has custody of all wills admitted to probate in England and Wales since 1858

[237] **General Register Office (Scotland)**
New Register House, Edinburgh EH1 3YT
Tel 031-556 3952
Registrar General CM Glennie

● M-Th 9.30-4.30, F 9.30-4

Has custody of all statutory registers of births, marriages and deaths in Scotland since 1855 and of all Scottish parish registers earlier than 1855

[238] **General Register Office (Northern Ireland)**
Oxford House, 49-55 Chichester Street, Belfast BT1 4HL
Tel 0232 235211 ext 2329 and 2326
Registrar General R McMurray

M-F 9.30-3.30

Has custody of all statutory registers of births, marriages and deaths in Northern Ireland since 1922

[239] **General Registry (Isle of Man)**
Finch Road, Douglas, Isle of Man
Tel 0624 75506
Chief Registrar P Curtis

M-F 9-1 2.15-4.30

Has custody of all statutory registers of births and deaths in the Isle of Man since 1878, marriages since 1883 and records of Church of England baptisms, marriages and burials earlier than these dates. Also maintains the Deeds Registry of wills admitted to probate and deeds since 1910

[240] **Greffe (Guernsey)**
Royal Court House, Guernsey
Tel 0481 25277
HM Greffier K Tough

● M-F 9-1 2-4
Repair

Has custody of the records of the Royal Court, the States of Guernsey, statutory registers of births, marriages and deaths since 1840, wills since 1841, deeds since 1576 and some private collections

List of records in the Greffe, Guernsey, 2 vols, 1969, 1978

[241] **Judicial Greffe (Jersey)**
States Building, 10 Hill Street, Royal Square, St Helier, Jersey
Tel 0534 75472
Judicial Greffier JE LeCornu
Registrar of Deeds PJ Bisson

M-F 10-1 2-5

Has custody of the records of the Royal Court and of the Public Registry of Deeds and the Probate Registry. Also houses the records of the States Assembly and Ecclesiastical Court and the statutory registers of births, marriages and deaths since 1842

Other Useful Addresses

The following organisations may be able to help students to locate specific record material:

[242] The Royal Commission on Historical Manuscripts
Quality House, Quality Court, Chancery Lane, London WC2A 1HP
Tel 01-242 1198
Secretary BS Smith

M-F 9.30-5

Acts as a central clearing-house for information about the nature and location of historical manuscripts and papers outside the public records. The National Register of Archives, the Manorial Documents Register and the Tithe Documents Register are available for public use in its search room. Its publications, which include an annual list of *Accessions to Repositories and Reports added to the National Register of Archives*, are comprehensively listed in HMSO *Government Publications Sectional List 17, Publications of the Royal Commission on Historical Manuscripts*, 1985

[243] Army Museums Ogilby Trust
Connaught Barracks, Duke of Connaught's Road, Aldershot GU11 2LR
Tel 0252 24431 ext 2895
Secretary Colonel PS Newton

M-F 9.30-5

Acts as a general clearing-house for information about the contents of all regimental and other military museums

[244] British Records Association
Master's Court, The Charterhouse, Charterhouse Square, London EC1M 6AU
Tel 01-253 0436
Hon Secretary TR Padfield

Due to move from this address in summer 1987

Exists to promote and encourage the work of all individuals and institutions interested in the conservation and use of records. Its Records Preservation Section arranges the deposit in appropriate repositories of documents received mainly from the offices of London solicitors

[245] Business Archives Council
185 Tower Bridge Road, London SE1 2UF
Tel 01-407 6110
Secretary General Ms SMR Kelly

Offers help in tracing the records of individuals industrial and commercial undertakings and guidance to the undertakings themselves on the management of their records

[246] Business Archives Council of Scotland
Glasgow University Archives, The University, Glasgow G12 8QQ
Tel 041-339 8855 ext 5515/6
Surveying Officer D Ashman

Performs similar functions to the Business Archives Council in England

[247] Church House Record Centre
Church House, Dean's Yard, London SW1P 3NZ
Tel 01-222 9011 ext 203
Archivist Mrs BL Hough

● M-F 10-5

Acts as a general clearing-house for information on all central records of the Church of England

[248] Society of Genealogists
14 Charterhouse Buildings, London EC1M 7BA
Tel 01-251 8799
Director and Secretary AJ Camp

T, F, S 10-6, W, Th 10-8. Closed one week in February

Its genealogical reference library is open to non-members on payment of a fee. Holds lists of the names and addresses of regional genealogical societies and of individual professional research workers in this field

Index

The references are to entry numbers

Aberdeen City Archives 211
Aberdeen University Library 212
Archive of Art & Design 70
Argyll and Bute District Archives 223
Army Museums Ogilby Trust 243
Ayrshire Subregion Archives 222

Barnet Local History Library 74
Barnsley Archive Service 178
Bath City Record Office 1
Bedfordshire Record Office 4
Berkshire Record Office 5
Berwick upon Tweed Record Office 241
Bexley Libraries Department 75
Bilston Branch Library 136
Birmingham Archives Department 132
Birmingham University Library 137
Bodleian Library 146
Bolton Archive Service 117
Borthwick Institute of Historical Research 176
Brent Leisure Services 76
Bristol Record Office 2
Bristol University Library 3
British Architectural Library 99
British Geological Survey Library 143
British Library:
  Department of Western Manuscripts 58
  India Office Library and Records 59
British Museum (Natural History) 60
British Records Association 244
Bromley Public Libraries 77
Brotherton Library 188
Buckinghamshire Archaeological Society 9
Buckinghamshire Record Office 8
Bury Archive Service 118
Business Archives Council 245
Business Archives Council of Scotland 246

Cambridge University:
  Library 12
  Archives 12
  Centre of South Asian Studies 13
  Churchill Archives Centre 14
  Scott Polar Research Institute 15
  Trinity College Library 16
Cambridgeshire Record Office 10–11
Camden Public Libraries 78
Canterbury Cathedral, City and Diocesan Record Office 54

Caernarfon Area Record Office 200
Cardiganshire Area Record Office 194
Carmarthenshire Area Record Office 193
Central Regional Council Archives Department 205
Cheshire Record Office 17
Chester City Record Office 18
Church House Record Centre 247
Cleveland County Archives Department 20
Clwyd Record Office 190–191
Contemporary Medical Archives Centre 112
Cornwall Record Office 21
Coventry City Record Office 133
Cumbria Record Office 23–25

Darlington Library 31
Derbyshire Record Office 26
Devon Record Office 27–28
Dolgellau Area Record Office 201
Doncaster Archives Department 179
Dorset Record Office 30
Dudley Archives and Local History Department 134
Dumfries Archive Centre 207
Dumfries and Galloway Regional Library Service 206
Dundee District Archive and Record Centre 229
Dundee University Library 232
Durham County Record Office 31
Durham Dean and Chapter Library 34
Durham University:
  Library 32
  Department of Palaeography and Diplomatic 33
Dyfed Archive Service 193–195

Edinburgh City Archives 217
Edinburgh University:
  Library 218
  New College Library 218
Essex Record Office 35–37
Exeter Cathedral Library 27, 29
Exeter University Library 29

Fawcett Library 98

Gateshead Central Library 167
General Register Office (Northern Ireland) 238
General Register Office (Scotland) 237
General Registry (Isle of Man) 239
Glamorgan Archive Service 196–197
Glasgow: Mitchell Library 224

Glasgow University:
  Library 225
  Archives 226
  Adam Smith Business Record Centre 226
Gloucestershire Record Office 38
Grampian Regional Archives 209
Greenwich Local History Library 79
Guernsey: Greffe 240
Guildford Muniment Room 161
Gwent County Record Office 199
Gwynedd Archives and Museums Service 200–202

Hackney Archives Department 80
Hammersmith and Fulham Archives 81
Hampshire Record Office 39
Haringey Libraries Department 82
Hawarden: St Deiniol's Library 190
Hereford and Worcester Record Office 43–45
Hertfordshire Record Office 46
Highland Regional Archive 213
House of Lords Record Office 61
Hull University: Brynmor Jones Library 50
Humberside County Record Office 47–48
Hythe Town Archives 52

Imperial War Museum 62
India Office Library and Records 59
Institution of Civil Engineers 100
Institution of Electrical Engineers 101

Jersey: Judicial Greffe 241

Keele University Library 156
Kensington and Chelsea Libraries 83
Kent Archives Office 51–53
Kingston upon Hull City Record Office 49
Kingston upon Thames Muniment Room 160

Lambeth Archives Department 84
Lambeth Palace Library 102
Lancashire Record Office 55
Leeds University: Brotherton Library 188
Leicestershire Record Office 56
Lewisham Local History Centre 85
Lichfield Joint Record Office 155
Lincolnshire Archives Office 57
Linnean Society of London 103
Liverpool Record Office 127
Liverpool University:
  Sydney Jones Library 130
  Archives Unit 131
Llangefni Area Record Office 202
London: City of London Polytechnic, Fawcett Library 98

London, Corporation of, Records Office 72
London, Greater, Record Office 71
London: Guildhall Library 73
London University:
  Library 91
  British Library of Political and Economic Science 92
  Imperial College Archives 93
  Institute of Commonwealth Studies 94
  King's College London Library and Archives 95
  Liddell Hart Centre for Military Archives 95
  School of Oriental and African Studies Library 96
  University College London Manuscripts Room 97

Manchester Central Library 119
Manchester, Greater, Record Office 116
Manchester University: John Rylands Library 125
Manx Museum Library 234
Methodist Archives and Research Centre 125
Moray District Record Office 210

National Army Museum 63
National Art Library 70
National Library of Scotland 214
National Library of Wales 192
National Maritime Museum 64
National Museums and Galleries on Merseyside:
  Archives Department 126
  Maritime Records Centre 126
National Railway Museum Library 174
National Register of Archives 242
National Register of Archives (Scotland) 216
Newcastle upon Tyne University Library 168
Norfolk Record Office 139
Northamptonshire Record Office 140
Northumberland Record Office 141
Nottingham University Library 144
Nottinghamshire Record Office 142

Office of Population Censuses and Surveys 235
Orkney Archives 220
Oxford University:
  Bodleian Library 146
  Archives 146
  Nuffield College Library 147
  Pusey House Library 148
  Rhodes House Library 146
  St Antony's College, Middle East Centre 149
Oxfordshire County Record Office 145

Pembrokeshire Area Record Office 195
Perth and Kinross District Archive 230
Perth Museum and Art Gallery 231
Portsmouth City Records Office 40
Powys Archives 204
Principal Registry of the Family Division 236
Public Record Office 65
Public Record Office of Northern Ireland 233

Reading University:
  Library 6
  Institute of Agricultural History 7
Redbridge Central Library 86
Rochdale Libraries Local Studies Department 120
Rotherham: Brian O'Malley Library 180
Royal Air Force Museum 66
Royal Astronomical Society Library 104
Royal Botanic Garden, Edinburgh 215
Royal Botanic Gardens Library, Kew 67
Royal College of Physicians of London 105
Royal College of Physicians and Surgeons of Glasgow 228
Royal College of Surgeons of England 106
Royal Commission on Historical Manuscripts 242
Royal Commonwealth Society Library 107
Royal Greenwich Observatory 163
Royal Institution of Cornwall 22
Royal Institution of Great Britain 108
Royal Society 109
Rylands, John, University Library of Manchester 125

St Andrews University Library 208
St Helens Local History and Archives Library 128
Salford Archives Centre 121
Science Museum Library 68
Scottish Catholic Archives 219
Scottish Record Office 216
Shakespeare Birthplace Trust Records Office 170
Sheffield Record Office 181
Sheffield University Library 182
Shetland Archives 221
Shropshire Libraries Local Studies Department 151
Shropshire Record Office 150
Society of Antiquaries of London 110
Society of Friends' Library 111
Society of Genealogists 248
Somerset Record Office 152
Southampton City Record Office 41

Southampton University Library 42
Southwark Local Studies Library 87
Stafford: William Salt Library 154
Staffordshire Record Office 153
Stockport Archive Service 122
Strathclyde Regional Archives 222
Strathclyde University Archives 227
Suffolk Record Office 157–159
Surrey Record Office 160–161
Sussex, East, Record Office 162
Sussex University Library 164
Sussex, West, Record Office 165
Swansea, University College of, Library 198

Tameside Local Studies Library 123
Tate Gallery Archive 69
Tayside Region 229
Tower Hamlets Libraries 88
Tyne and Wear Archives Service 166

Victoria & Albert Museum Library 70

Wales, University of:
  University College of North Wales Library 203
  University College of Swansea Library 198
Walsall Archives Service 135
Waltham Forest Archives 89
Warrington Library 19
Warwick County Record Office 169
Warwick University Modern Records Centre 138
Wellcome Institute for the History of Medicine 112
Westminster Abbey Muniment Room and Library 113
Westminster City Libraries 90
Westminster Diocesan Archives 114
Wigan Record Office 124
Wight, Isle of, County Record Office 171
Williams's, Dr, Library 115
Wiltshire Record Office 172
Wirral Archives Service 129
Wolverhampton Borough Archives 136
Worcester Dean and Chapter 137
Worcester (St Helen's) Record Office 45

York City Archives Department 175
York Minster Library 177
York University: Borthwick Institute of Historical Research 176
Yorkshire Archaeological Society 189
Yorkshire, North, County Record Office 173
Yorkshire, South, County Record Office 181
Yorkshire, West, Archives 183–187